Change Leadership

Developing a Change-Adept Organization

MARTIN ORRIDGE

GOWER

Published by
Gower Publishing Limited
Wey Court East
Union Road
Farnham
Surrey, GU9 7PT
England

Ashgate Publishing Company
Suite 420
101 Cherry Street
Burlington,
VT 05401-4405
USA

www.gowerpublishing.com

British Library Cataloguing in Publication Data
Orridge, Martin, 1947-
   Change leadership : developing a change adept organization.
   1. Organizational change. 2. Personnel management.
   3. Employees--Attitudes.
   I. Title
   658.4'06-dc22

   ISBN: 978-0-566-08935-0

Library of Congress Control Number: 2009924483

Mixed Sources
Product group from well-managed
forests and other controlled sources
www.fsc.org Cert no. SA-COC-1565
© 1996 Forest Stewardship Council
FSC

Printed and bound in Great Britain by
MPG Books Group, UK